# TIM JEFFS ART
## Animal Sketches
# *Rainforest*
# Birds

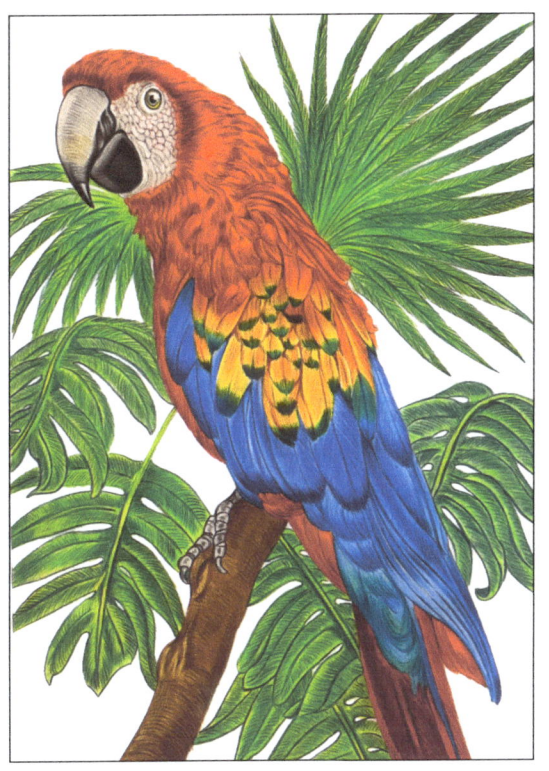

## A Special Edition Coloring Book

For Jane, Jenna and Harrison

Dedicated to all of the wonderful colorists who have supported my art and made my drawings more beautiful with their colors, and all the precious creatures that we live among.
A special thank you to Jo Warren for all of her continued support and beautiful colorings and lesson that make this book so much more special!

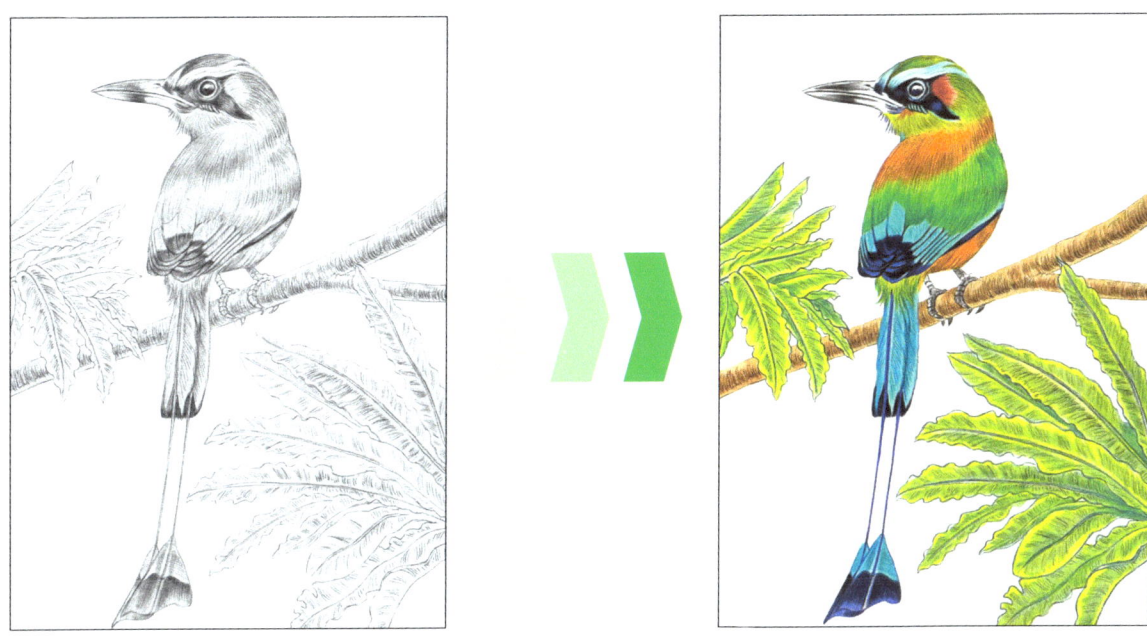

© Copyright 2021 Tim Jeffs Art
All rights reserved. No part of this publication may be reproduced or distributed in any form without the prior written permission of Tim Jeffs Art.

Tim Jeffs Art
376 East Madison Avenue, Dumont, NJ 07628

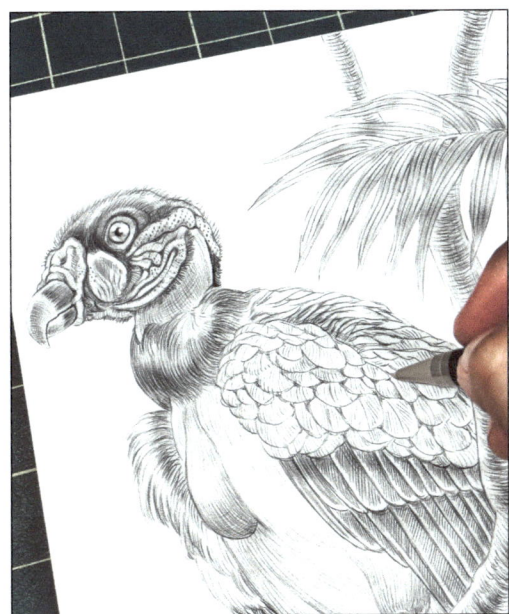 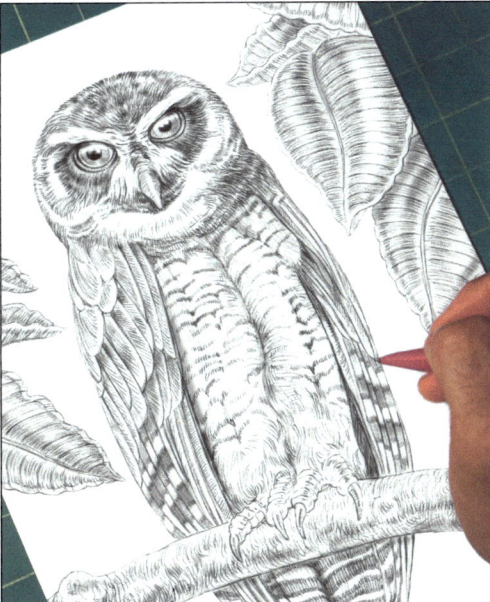 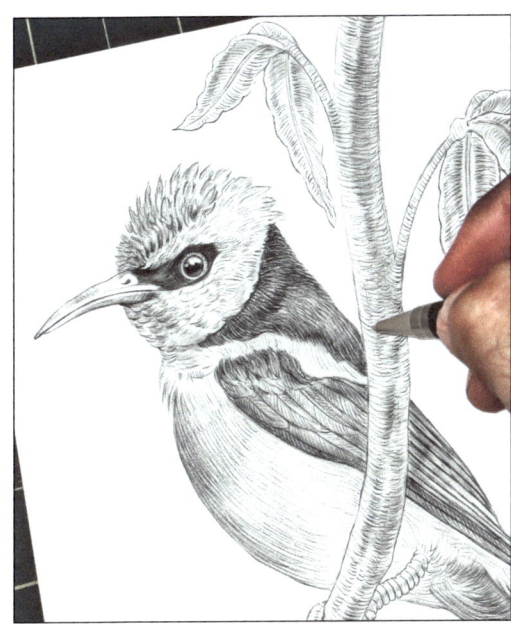

# Rainforest Birds Sketches Thoughts

**What's more colorful than the birds that inhabit the rainforests of the world? Not much!** Every color of the rainbow seems to adorn these majestic creatures. In this coloring book I wanted to highlight the beautiful birds that live in the rainforests around the world. From Central America to the Amazon and South East Asia, our rainforests are incredibly important diverse ecosystems that deserve protection of the animals and plants that live there. I encourage you to look these birds up online and see how spectacular their colors are. Though you may want to color them in their natural state, it's also fun to take artistic liberty and use your imagination to come up with your own colors.

In this coloring book for the first time I have included in my drawings the animals in an environment, including a variety of rainforest plants which will give you further coloring creativity options to have fun with.

I hope you enjoy coloring this group of rainforest bird sketches as much as I enjoyed drawing them, and I know that with your colors, you will bring these beautiful rainforest birds and the plants they live among to life!

**GRAYSCALE COLORING LESSON**
Keel-Billed Toucan

**Lesson level: Moderate**

# Coloring the
# Keel-Billed Toucan

On the next page I will walk you through the coloring of the Keel-Billed Toucan which is on page 4 of this coloring book. I had the pleasure to see this beautiful bird in it's natural habitat when I was vacationing with my family in Costa Rica. We were having a fun day of ziplining in the rainforest when a Keel-Billed Toucan landed in a tree a few yards from us. It was so colorful it almost looked unreal. This beautiful coloring of the Toucan was done by Jo Warren. Many thanks for her creative and inspirational step-by-step photos in the coloring lesson.

## ❯ Supply List

In this lesson, Faber Castell Polychromos pencils were used, (pencil numbers are listed below) but you can use any brand with similar colors.

1) **The coloring page can be found on page 4**
2) **Colors: Faber Castell Polychromos pencils:**

   171 Light Green
   112 Leaf Green
   168 Earth Green Yellowish
   105 Light Cadmium Yellow
   107 Cadmium Yellow
   115 Cadmium Orange
   118 Scarlett Red

   133 Magenta
   151 Helio Blue-Reddish
   152 Middle Pthhalo Blue
   180 Raw Umber
   225 Dark Red
   199 Black

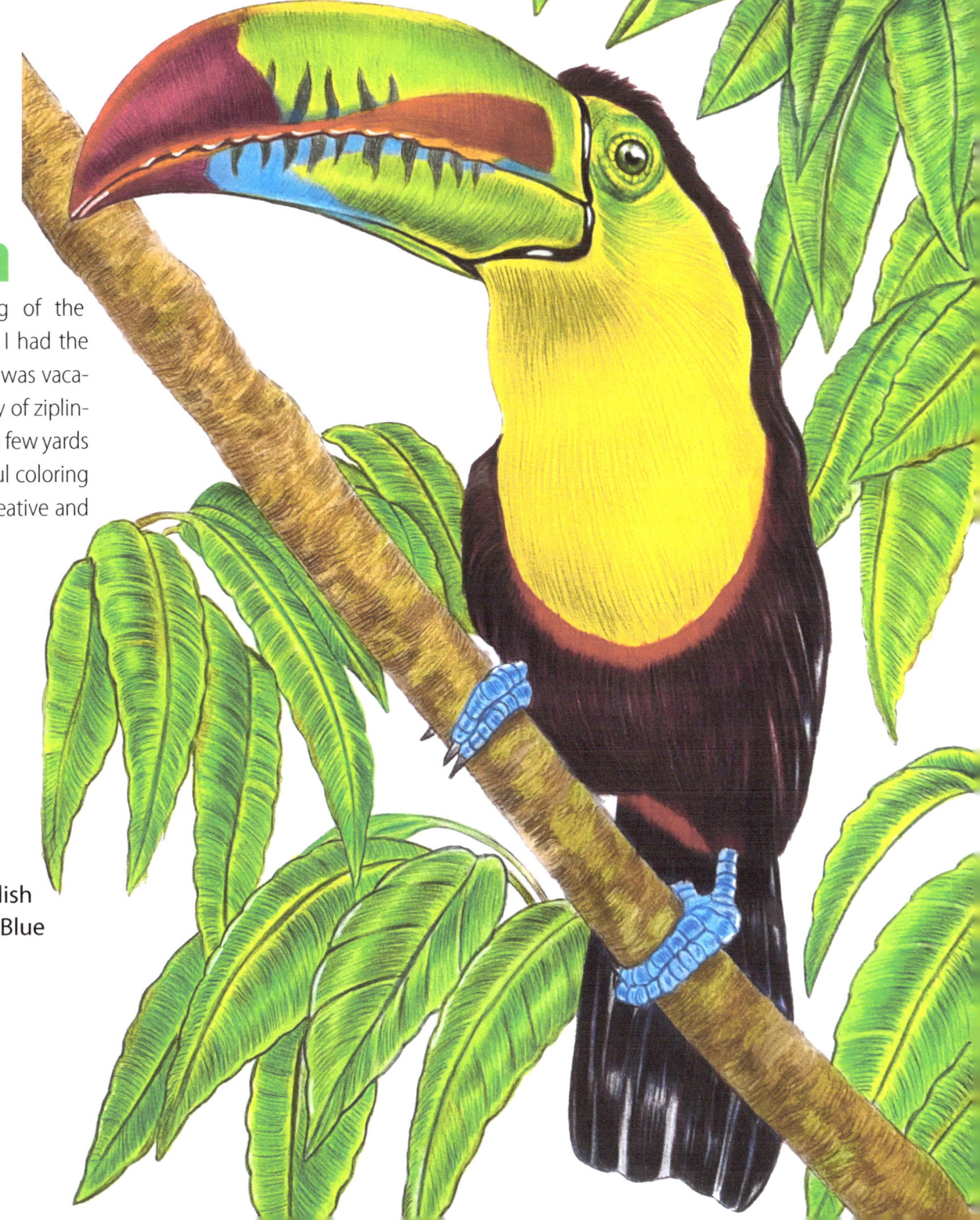

## GRAYSCALE COLORING LESSON
### Keel-Billed Toucan

# Keel-Billed Toucan
**Supplies needed:** A variety of colorful pencils

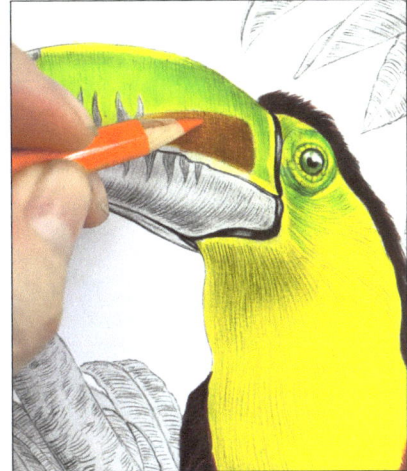

**Step 1.** Color the Toucan's neck, head and the top half of the beak with Light Cadmium Yellow (105). Layer over the head and beak with Leaf Green (112). Add Dark Cadmium Orange (115) to the rectangular beak ornamentation.

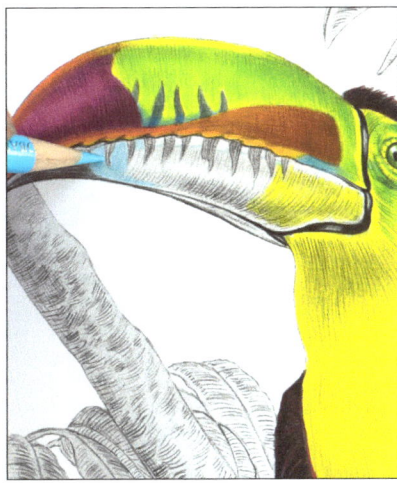

**Step 2.** Add Magenta (133) to the tip of the top and bottom beak. Color a V shape section of the lower beak in Middle Pthhalo Blue (152) and the rest of the lower beak in Yellow (105) with a top layer of Leaf Green (112).

You did it!
Your Keel-Billed Toucan is done!

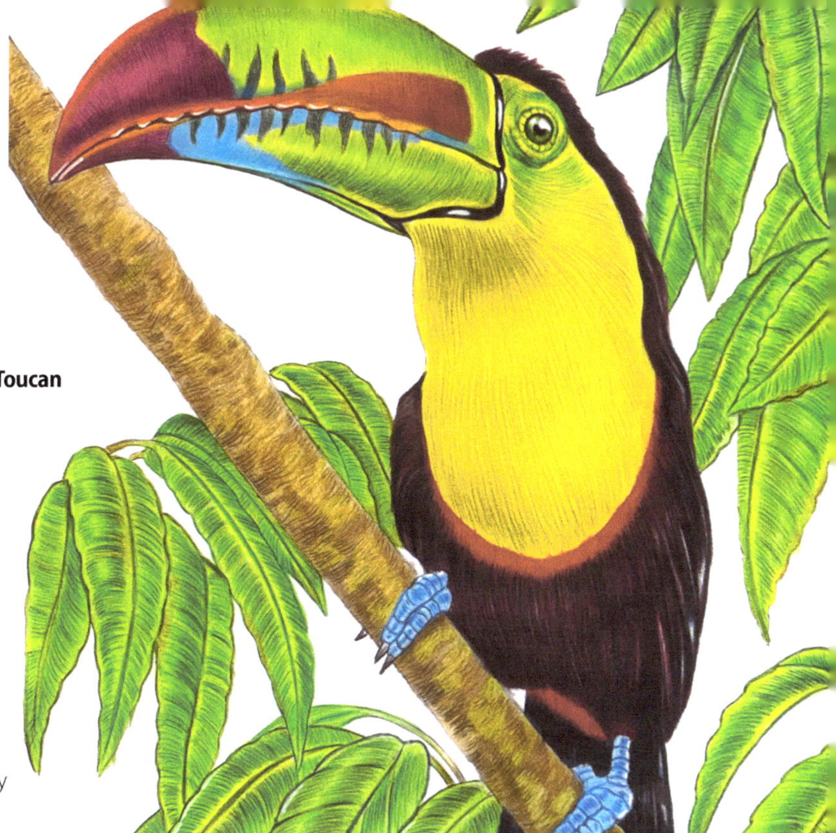

Coloring Steps by Jo Warren

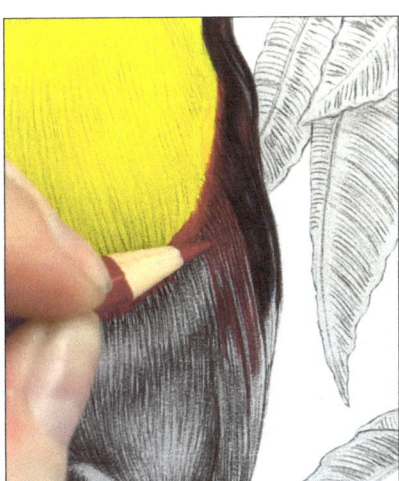

**Step 3.** Add Dark Red (225) to the body below the yellow neck. Next, leaving a stripe of full color Red at the top of the body, color over the rest of the Dark Red with lines of Black (199) letting some of the Dark Red show through.

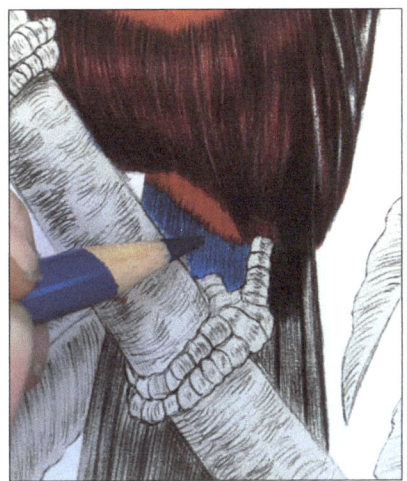

**Step 4.** Color the very top of the tail in Dark Red (225). Color the rest of the tail in Helio Blue-Redish (151). Color over the Blue with lines of Black (199) letting some of the Blue show through.

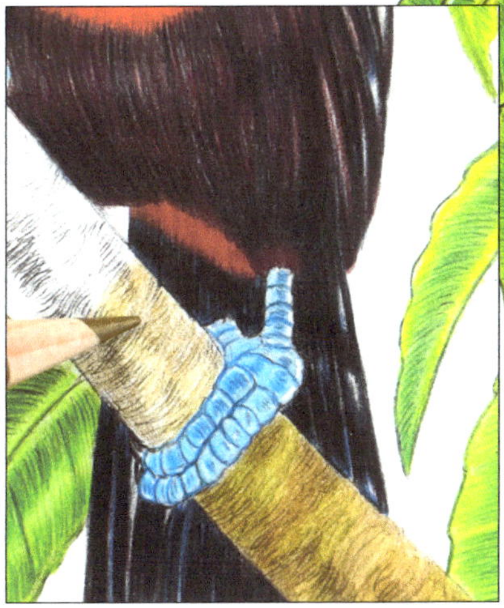

**Step 5** First color the Toucan's feet with a layer of Middle Pthhalo Blue (152) and darken the centers of the feet using Helio Blue-Redish (151). Color in the tree branch with Raw Umber (180) Dark Red (225) and Black (199).

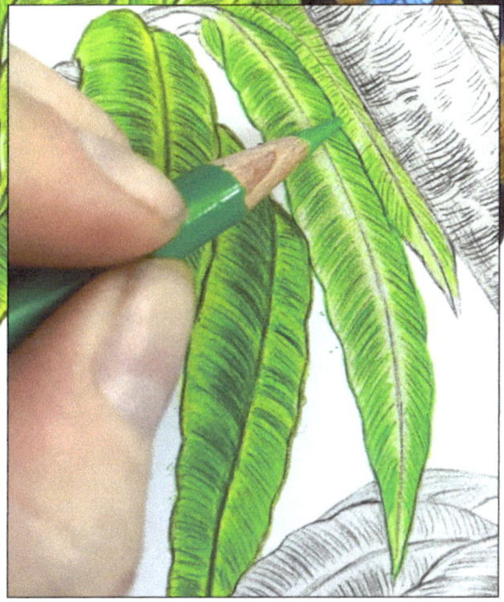

**Step 6.** Color the leaves with Leaf Green (112) and color the other edges with Light Cadmium Yellow (105). To give the leaves shape add lines of Earth Green Yellowish (168) from the center of the leaf outward toward the edges.

# Spreading Awareness through Coloring

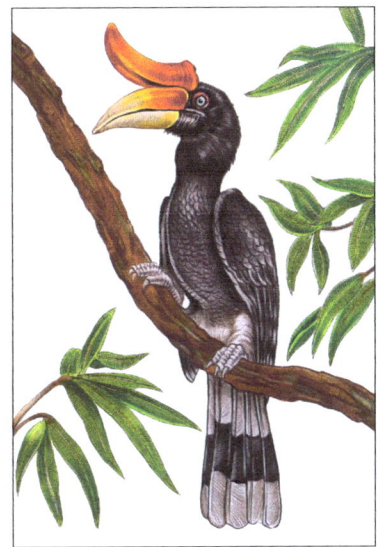

 **Rhinoceros Hornbill**
Vulnerable

**I truly believe that raising awareness through the sharing of my artwork** is a fantastic way to educate people about conservation. And coloring animals is a beautiful way to learn about them as you enjoy a relaxing and fun pastime. On the following page, I listed the Rainforest Birds statuses on the *International Union for Conservation of Nature's (IUCN)* conservation list. I think it's important to include the *(IUCN)* conservation list so people understand the classifications more clearly. To the right is an overview of the IUCN's conservation list, which breaks animals' conservation statuses into several categories. Knowing what these categories mean and the animals that are included in them is extremely important. **Together through art we can change the world!**

Tim Jeffs
Animal Artist

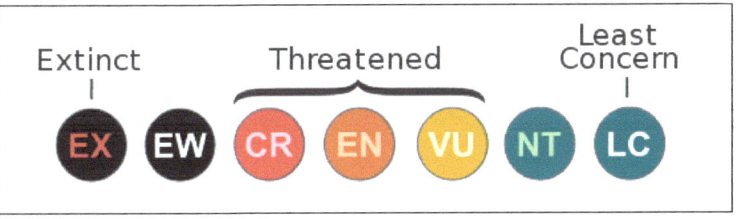

The list consists of 7 categories. From Least Concerned all the way to Extinct. Here are the definitions of each category:

- **LEAST CONCERN (LC):** A species that has been evaluated but not qualified for any other category on the list.
- **NEAR THREATENED (NT):** A species that may be considered threatened with extinction in the near future.
- **VULNERABLE (VU)**: A species likely to become endangered unless the circumstances that are threatening its survival and reproduction improve.
- **ENDANGERED (EN):** A species that is considered very likely to become extinct.
- **CRITICALLY ENDANGERED (CR):** A species that is facing an extremely high risk of becoming extinct in the wild.
- **EXTINCT IN THE WILD (EW):** A species that is only known by living members kept in captivity or as a naturalized population outside its historic range due to massive habitat loss.
- **EXTINCT (EX):** A species that has been terminated.

# Learn about the *Rainforest* Birds

Before you start coloring, it's important to learn where the birds in this book live and to know their conservation status.

### ❯ Chestnut-Colored Woodpecker
Found in Belize, Costa Rica, Guatemala, Honduras, Mexico, Nicaragua, and Panama.
**Conservation Status:** Least Concern

### ❯ Great Curassow
It's range is from eastern Mexico, through Central America to western Colombia and northwestern Ecuador. Threatened by loss of habitat and hunting.
**Conservation Status:** Vulnerable

### ❯ Hoatzin
Found in swamps, riparian forests, and mangroves of the Amazon and the Orinoco basins in South America.
**Conservation Status:** Least Concern

### ❯ Keel-Billed Toucan
Also known as sulfur-breasted toucan or rainbow-billed toucan it is found in the tropical jungles from southern Mexico to Colombia.
**Conservation Status:** Least Concern

### ❯ King Vulture
Found in Central and South America it lives in tropical lowland forests stretching from southern Mexico to northern Argentina.
**Conservation Status:** Least Concern

### ❯ Montezuma Oropendola
Iinhabits forest canopies in the Caribbean and Central America. Females build hanging woven nests of fibers and vines.
**Conservation Status:** Least Concern

### ❯ Red-Legged Honeycreeper
Inhabits southern Mexico south to Peru, Bolivia and central Brazil, Trinidad and Tobago, and Cuba.
**Conservation Status:** Least Concern

### ❯ Red-Tailed Comet
Can be found in the central Andes of Bolivia and Argentina, in Chile and in Peru.
**Conservation Status:** Least Concern

### ❯ Rhinoceros Hornbill
Found in lowland and montane, and in mountain rain forests in Borneo, Sumatra, Java, the Malay Peninsula, Singapore, and southern Thailand. It is threatened by loss of its rainforest habitat, as well as hunting for its skull and feathers.
**Conservation Status:** Vulnerable

### ❯ Rufous-Backed Dwarf Kingfisher
It is found in Brunei, India, Indonesia, Malaysia, the Philippines, and Thailand in tropical lowland forests.
**Conservation Status:** Least Concern

### ❯ Scarlet Macaw
It lives in evergreen forests of tropical Central and South America.
**Conservation Status:** Least Concern

### ❯ Speckled Tanager
It's range is from Costa Rica, Panama, Trinidad, Venezuela, Colombia, Guyana, Suriname and the extreme north of Brazil.
**Conservation Status:** Least Concern

### ❯ Spectacled Owl
It lives in forests from southern Mexico and Trinidad, through Central America, south to southern Brazil, Paraguay and northwestern Argentina.
**Conservation Status:** Least Concern

### ❯ Turquoise-Browed Motmot
It inhabits Central America from south-east Mexico (mostly the Yucatán Peninsula), to Costa Rica.
**Conservation Status:** Least Concern

### ❯ Wilson's Bird-Of-Paradise
Found in the lowland rainforests of Waigeo and Batanta Islands off West Papua. The first footage of the Wilson's bird-of-paradise ever to be filmed was recorded in 1996 by David Attenborough for a BBC documentary.
**Conservation Status:** Near Threatened

# Rainforest Birds Index

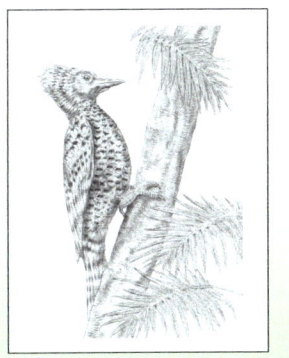
Chestnut-Colored Woodpecker 1

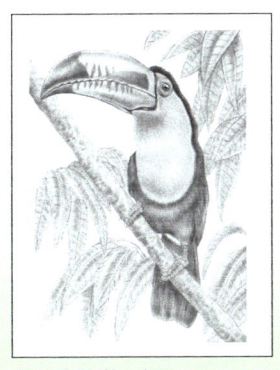
Keel-Billed Toucan 4

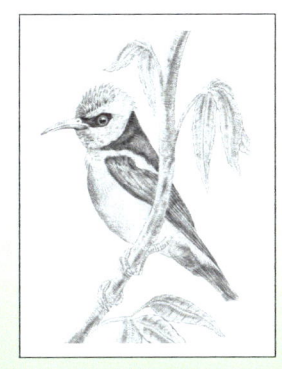
Red-Legged Honeycreeper 7

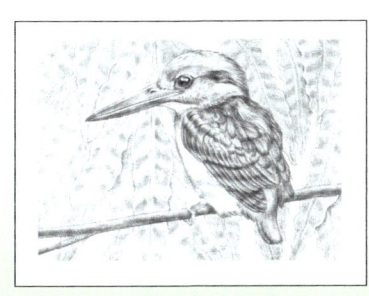
Rufous-Backed Kingfisher 10

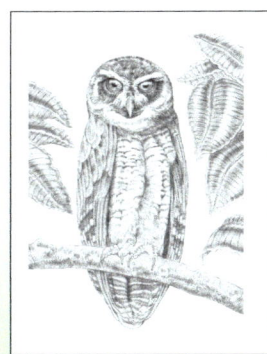
Spectacled Owl 13

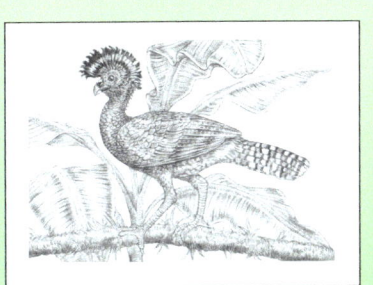
Great Curassow 2

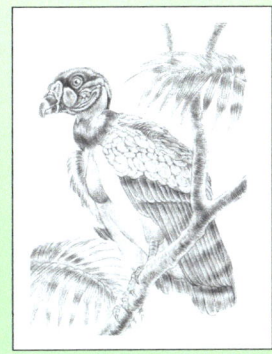
King Vulture 5

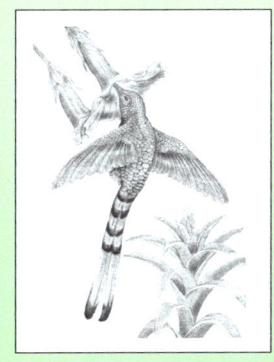
Red-Tailed Comet 8

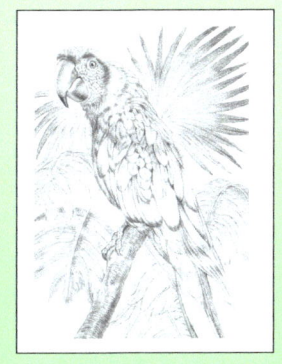
Scarlet Macaw 11

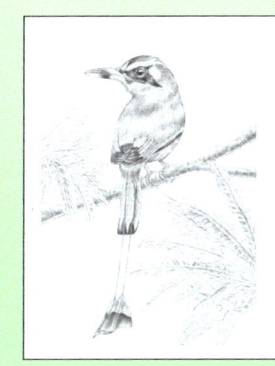
Turquoise-Browed Motmot 14

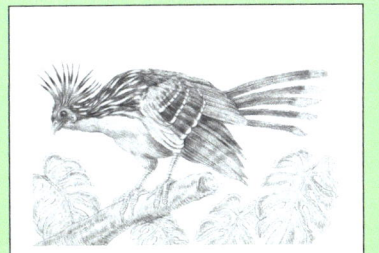
Hoatzin 3

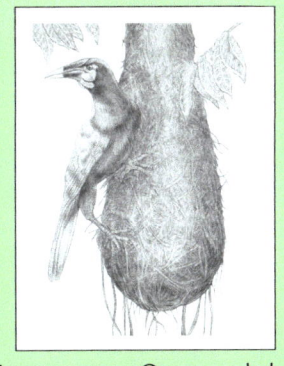
Montezuma Oropendola 6

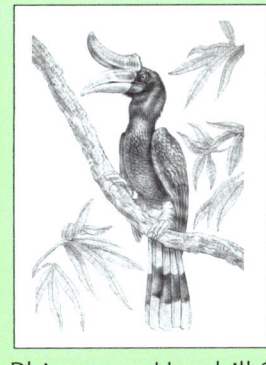
Rhinoceros Hornbill 9

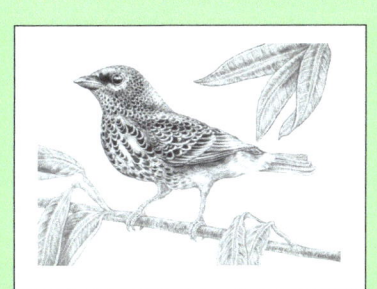
Speckled Tanager 12

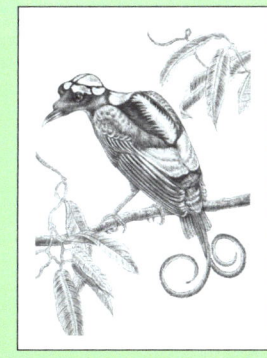
Wilson's Bird-of-Paradise 15

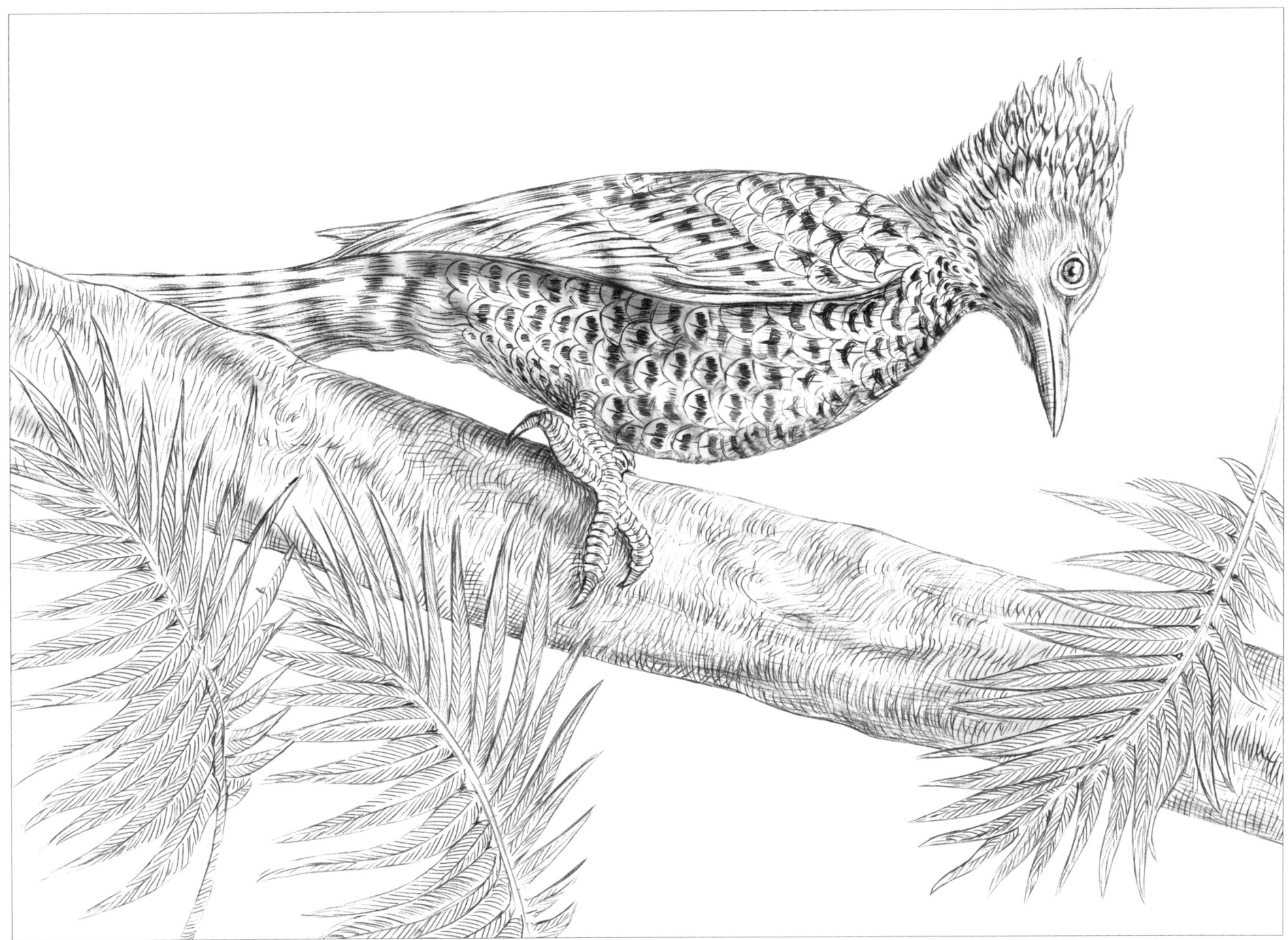

Chestnut-Colored Woodpecker

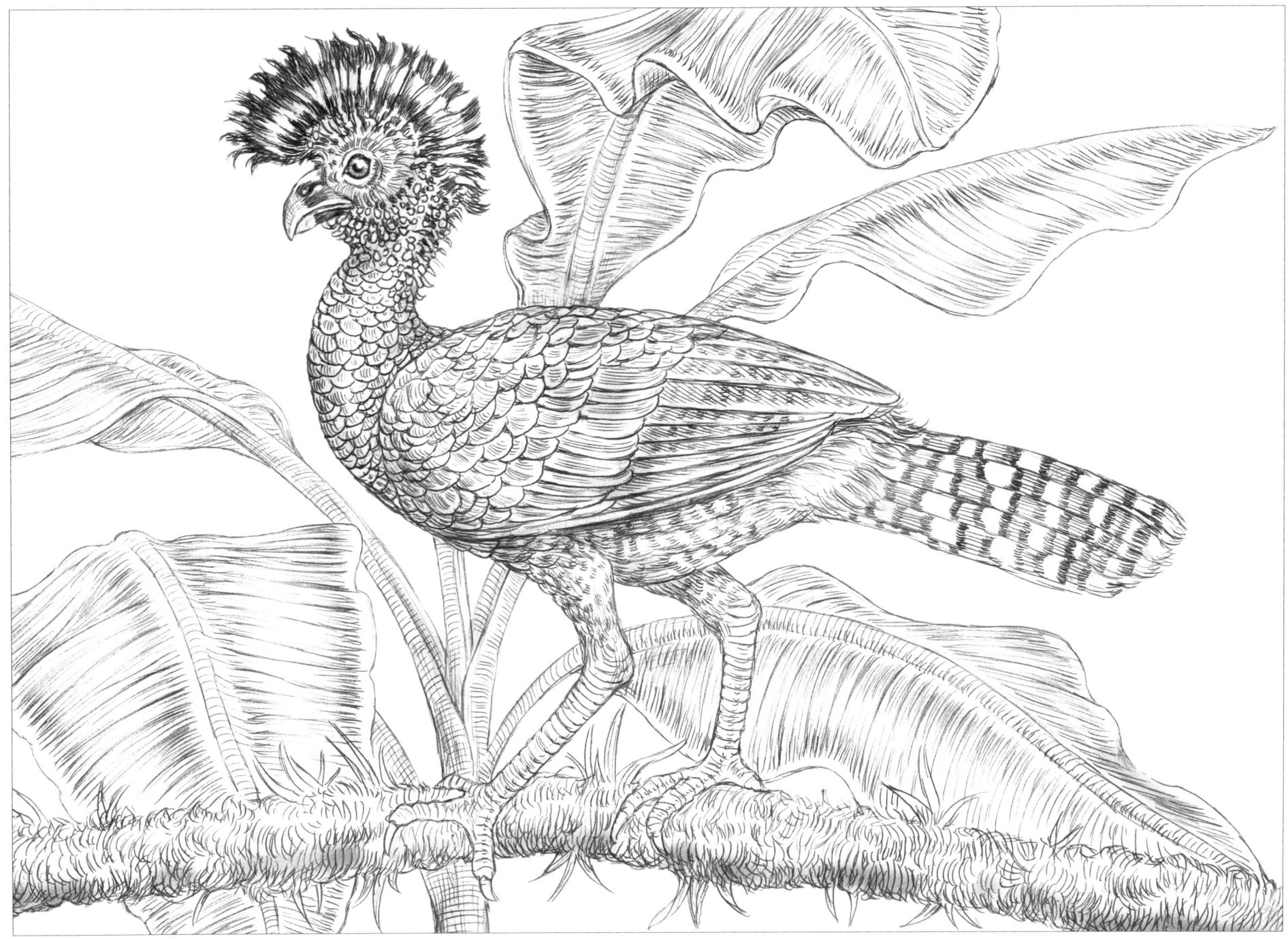

Great Curassow

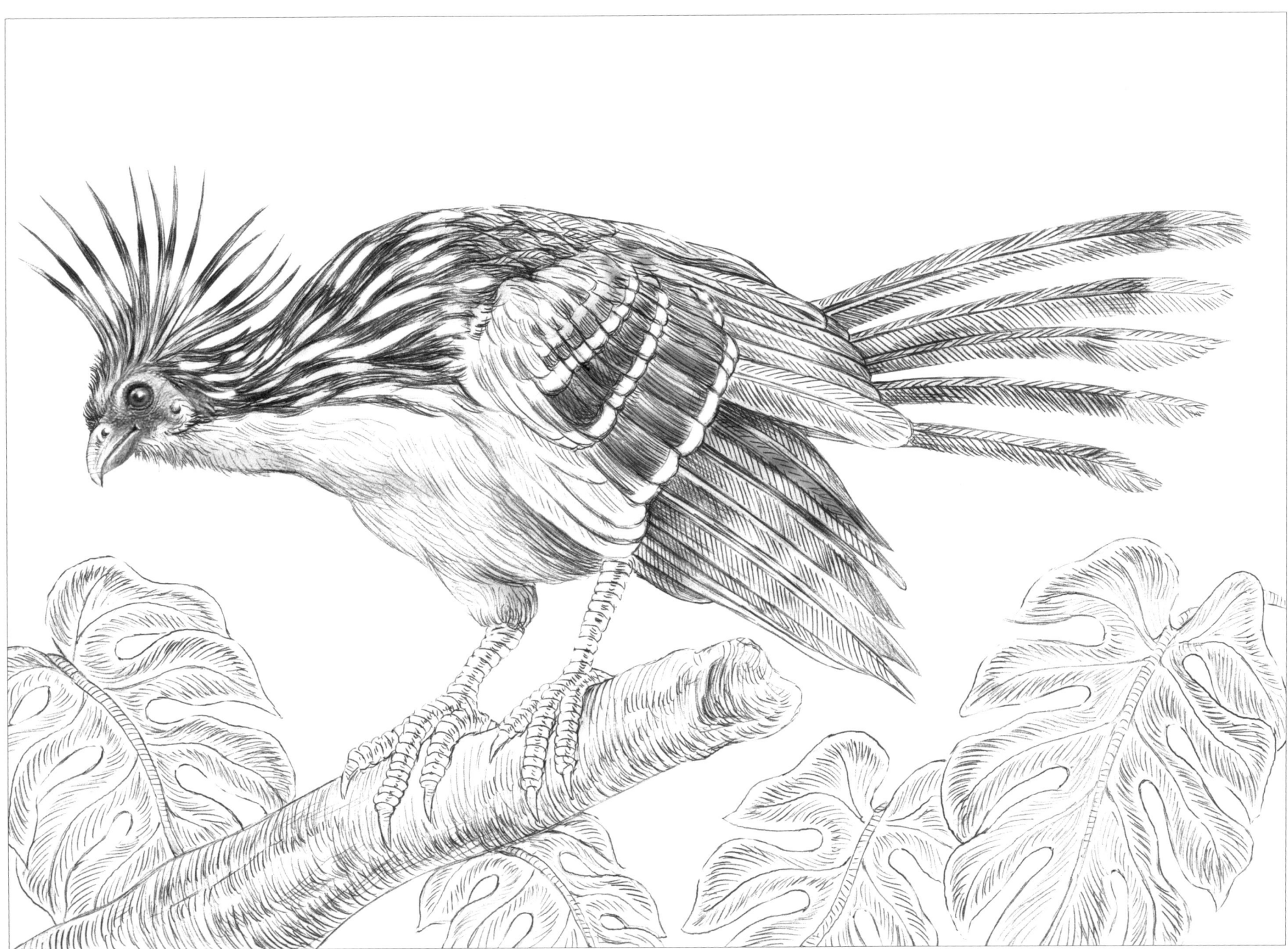

Hoatzin

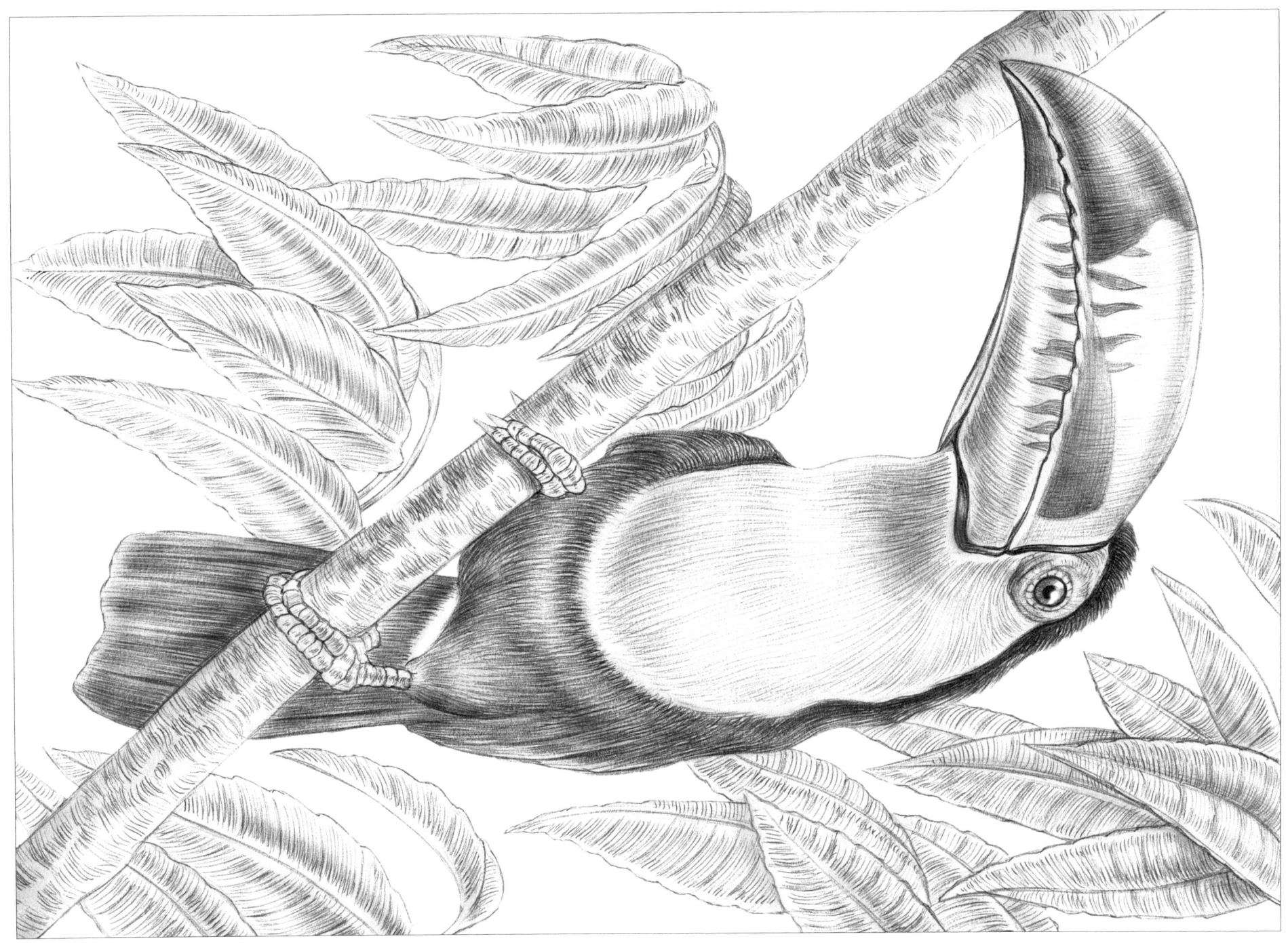

Keel-Billed Toucan

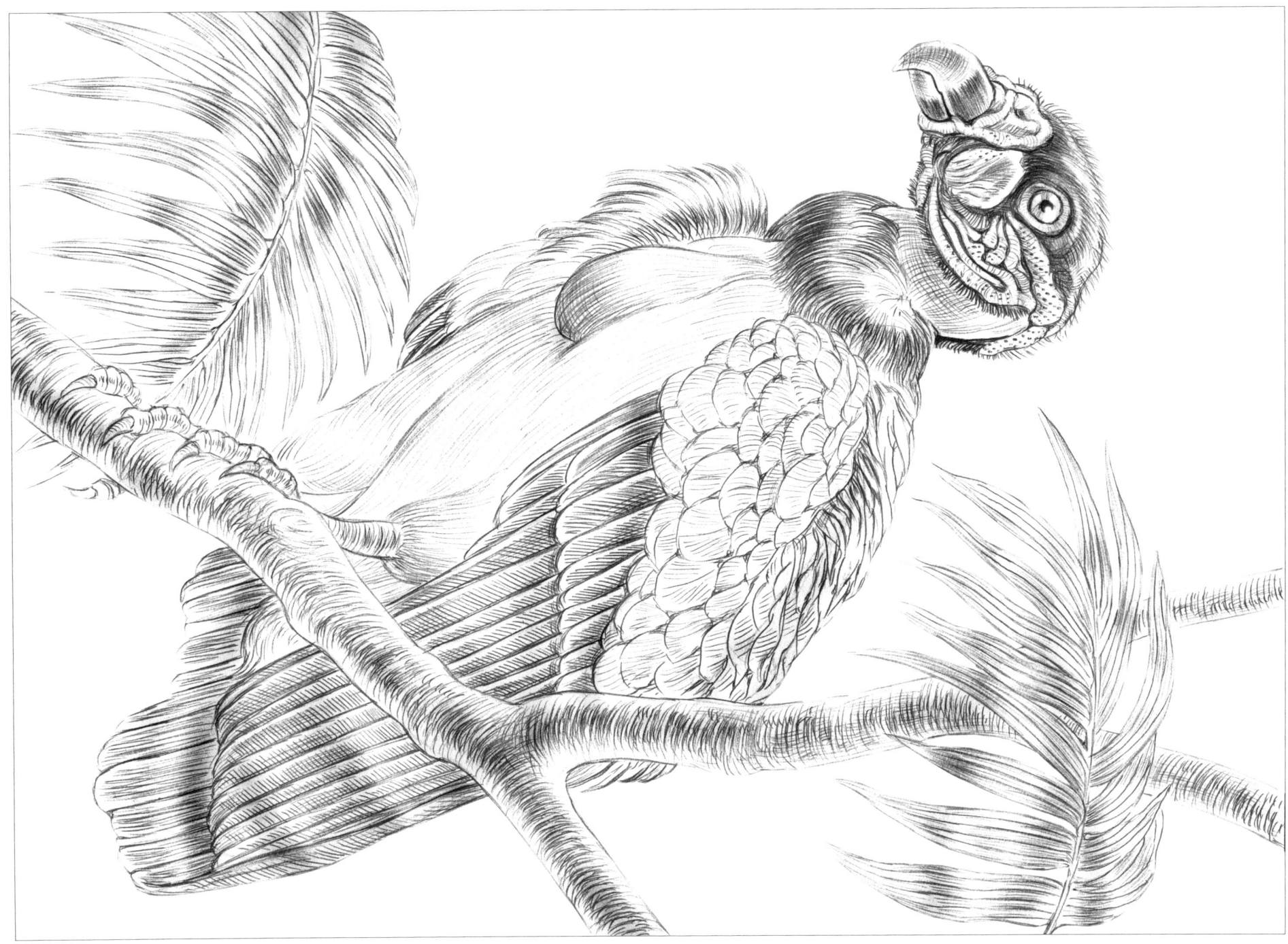

King Vulture

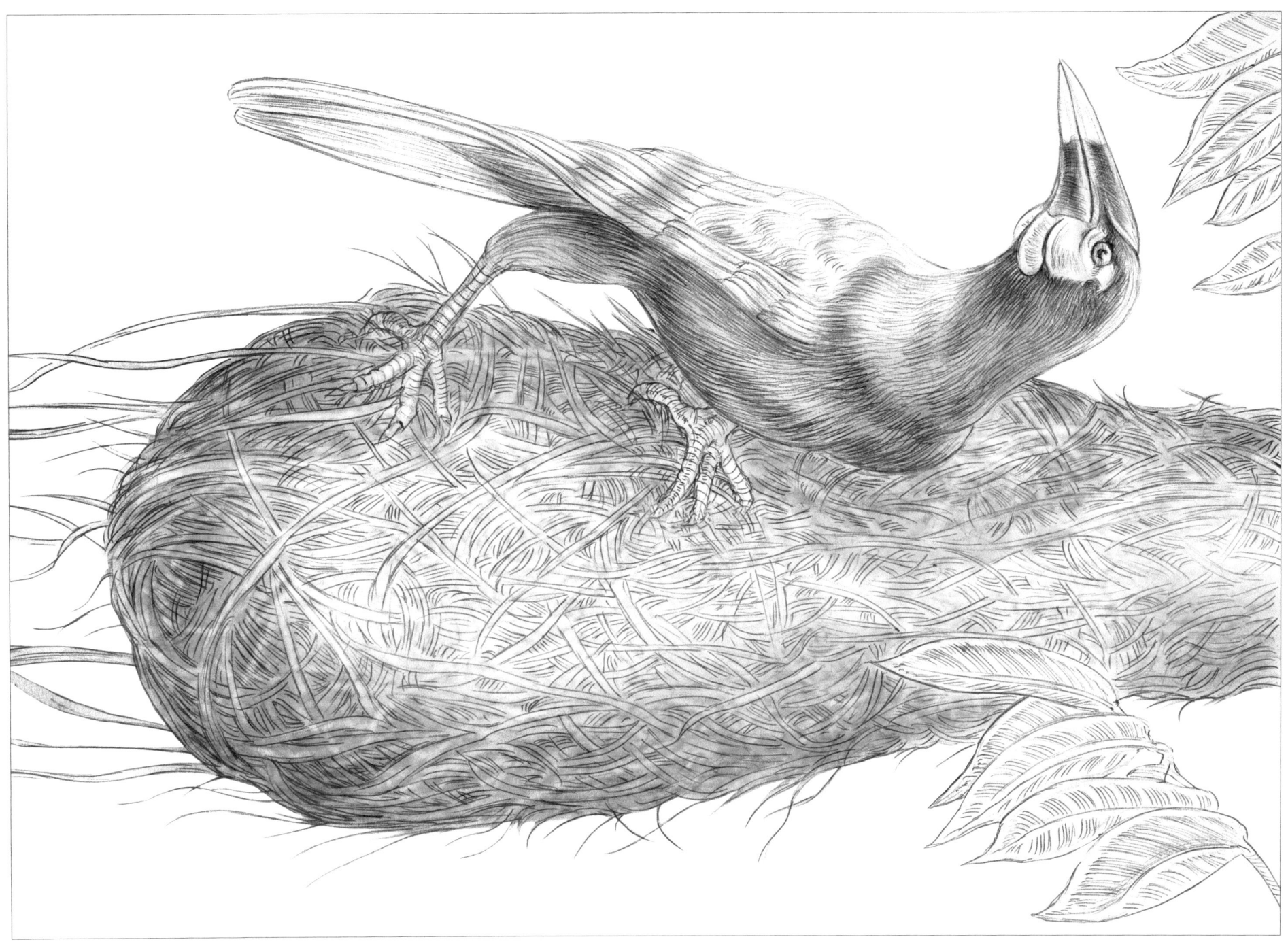

Montezuma Oropendola

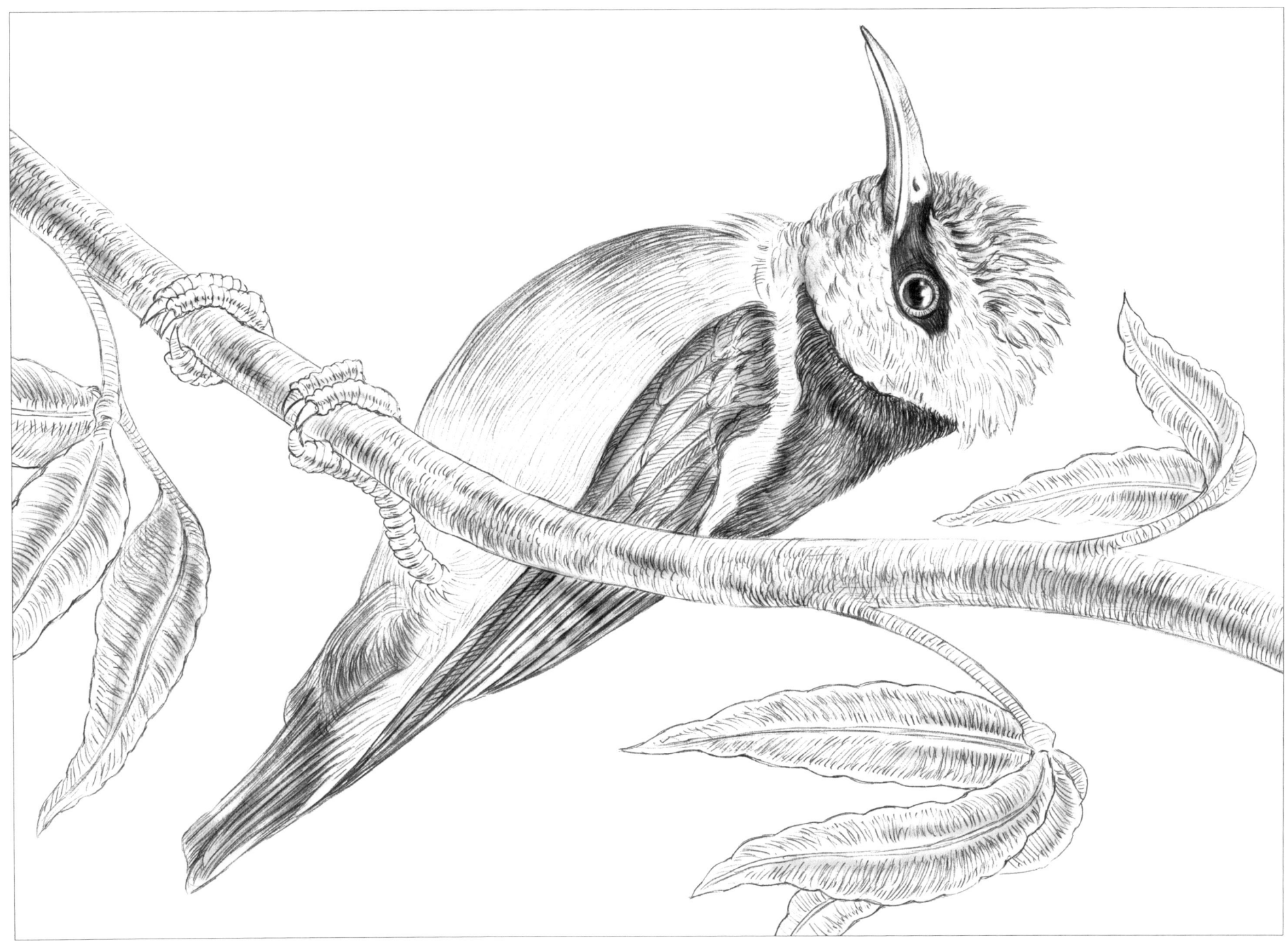

Red-Legged Honeycreeper

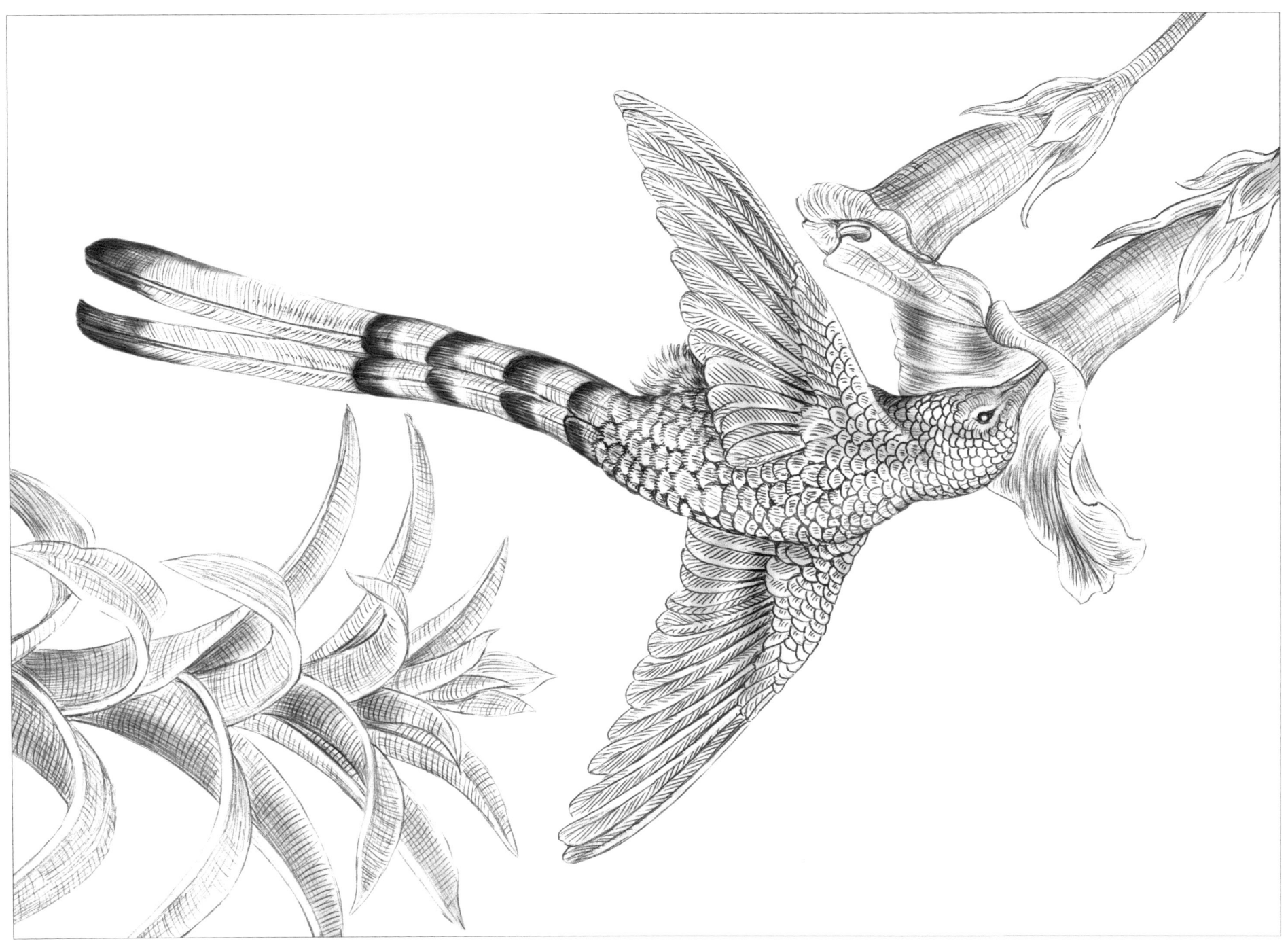

Red-Tailed Comet

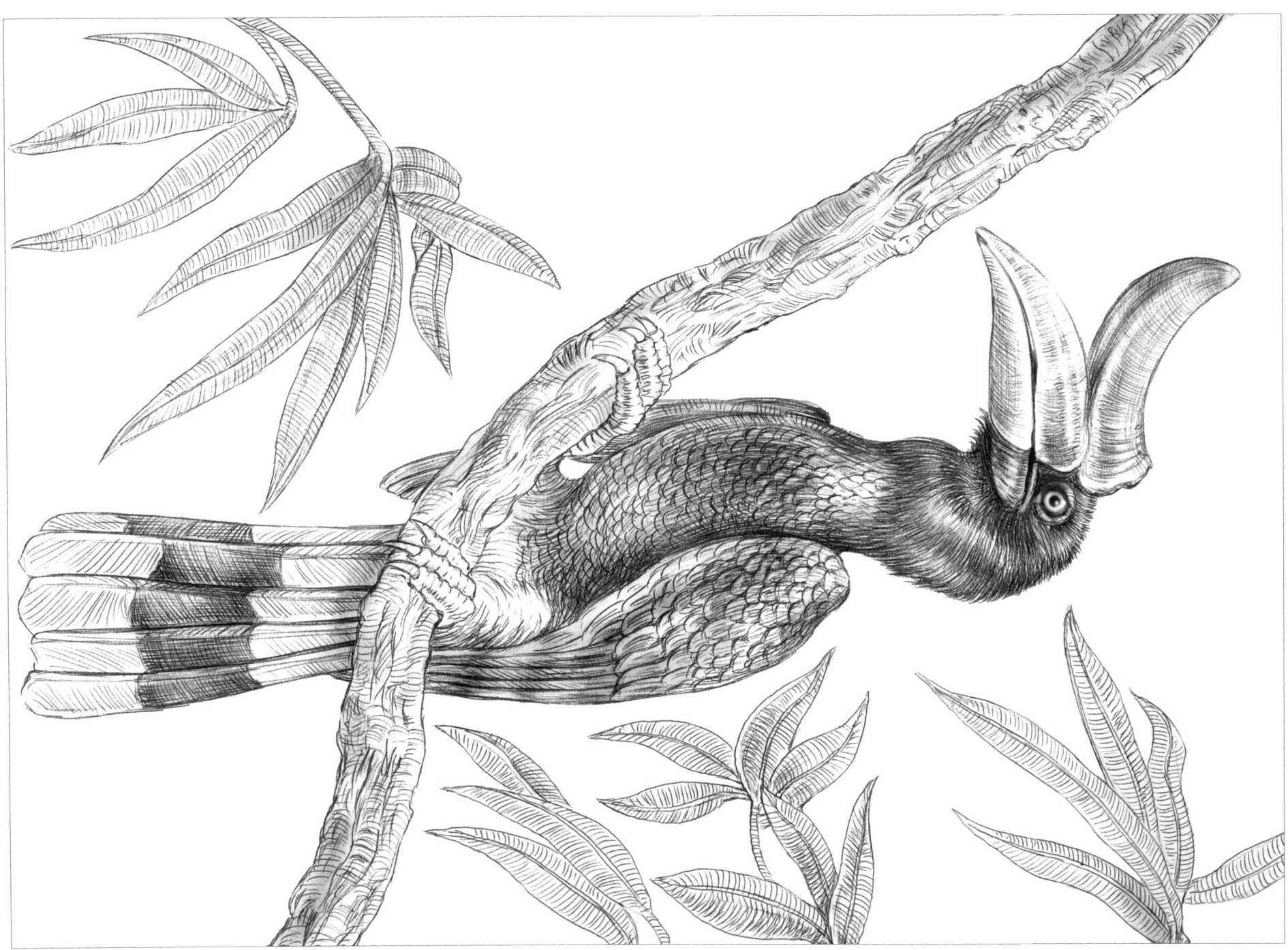

Rhinoceros Hornbill

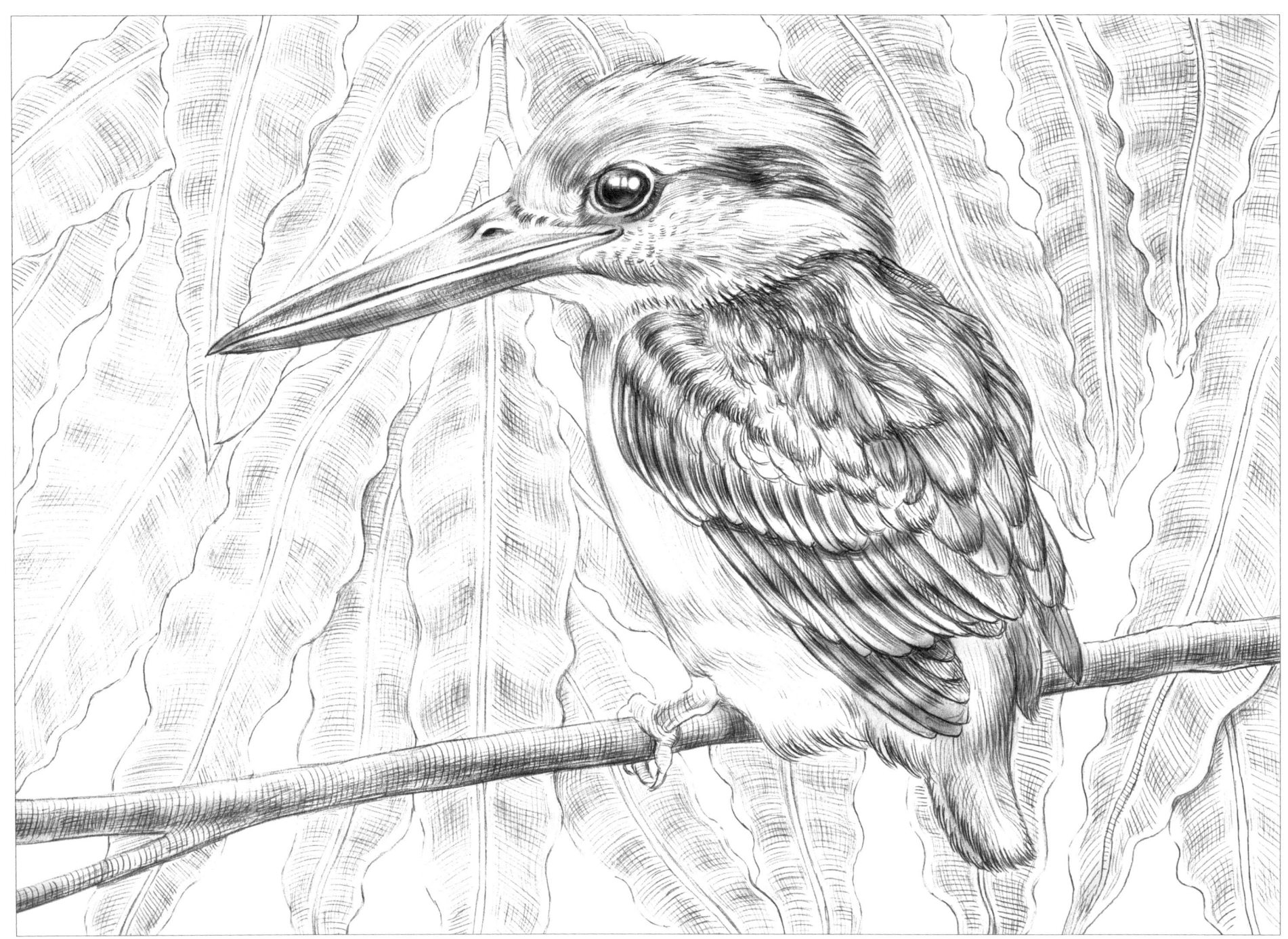

Rufous-Backed Kingfisher

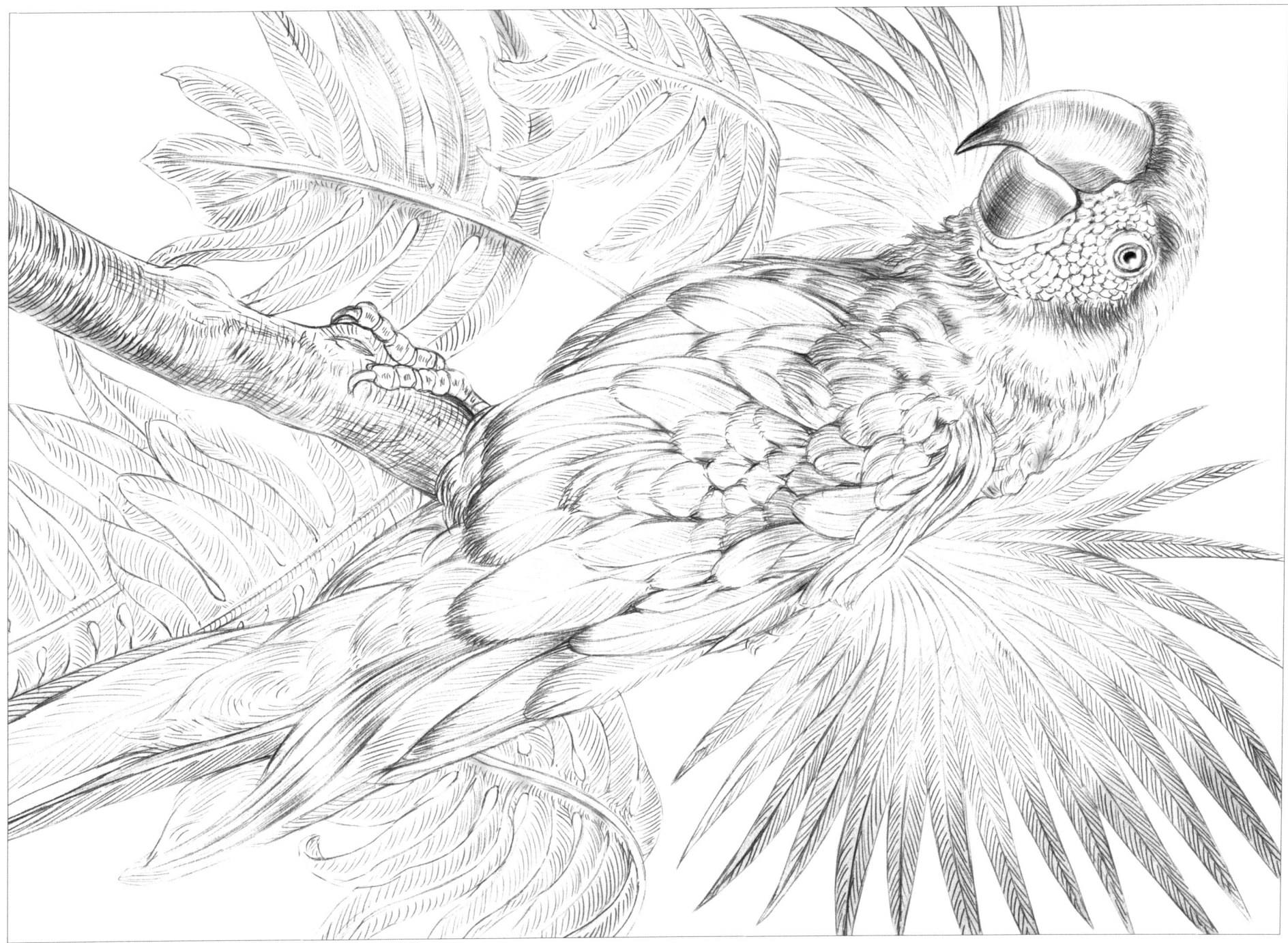

Scarlet Macaw

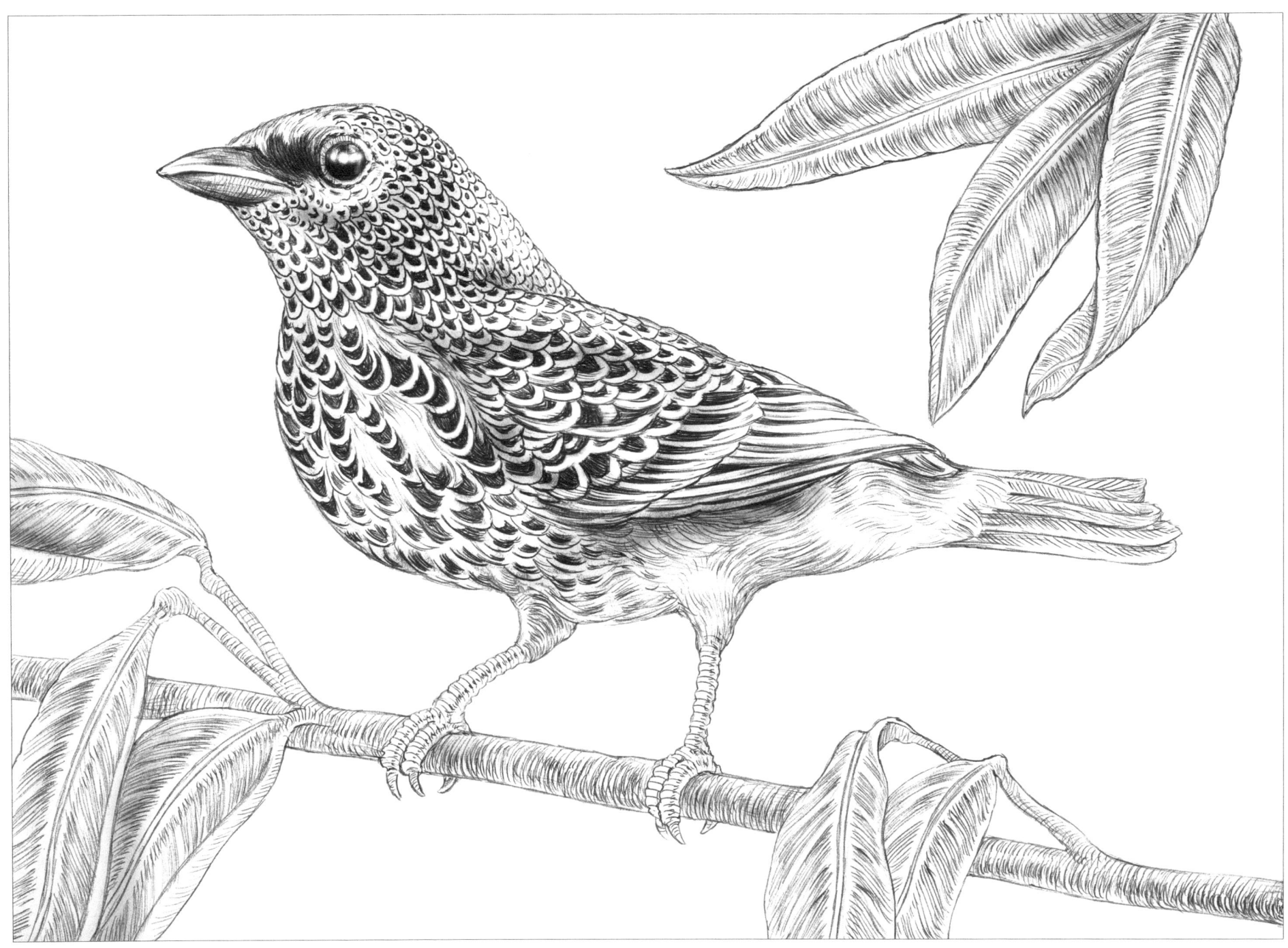

Speckled Tanager

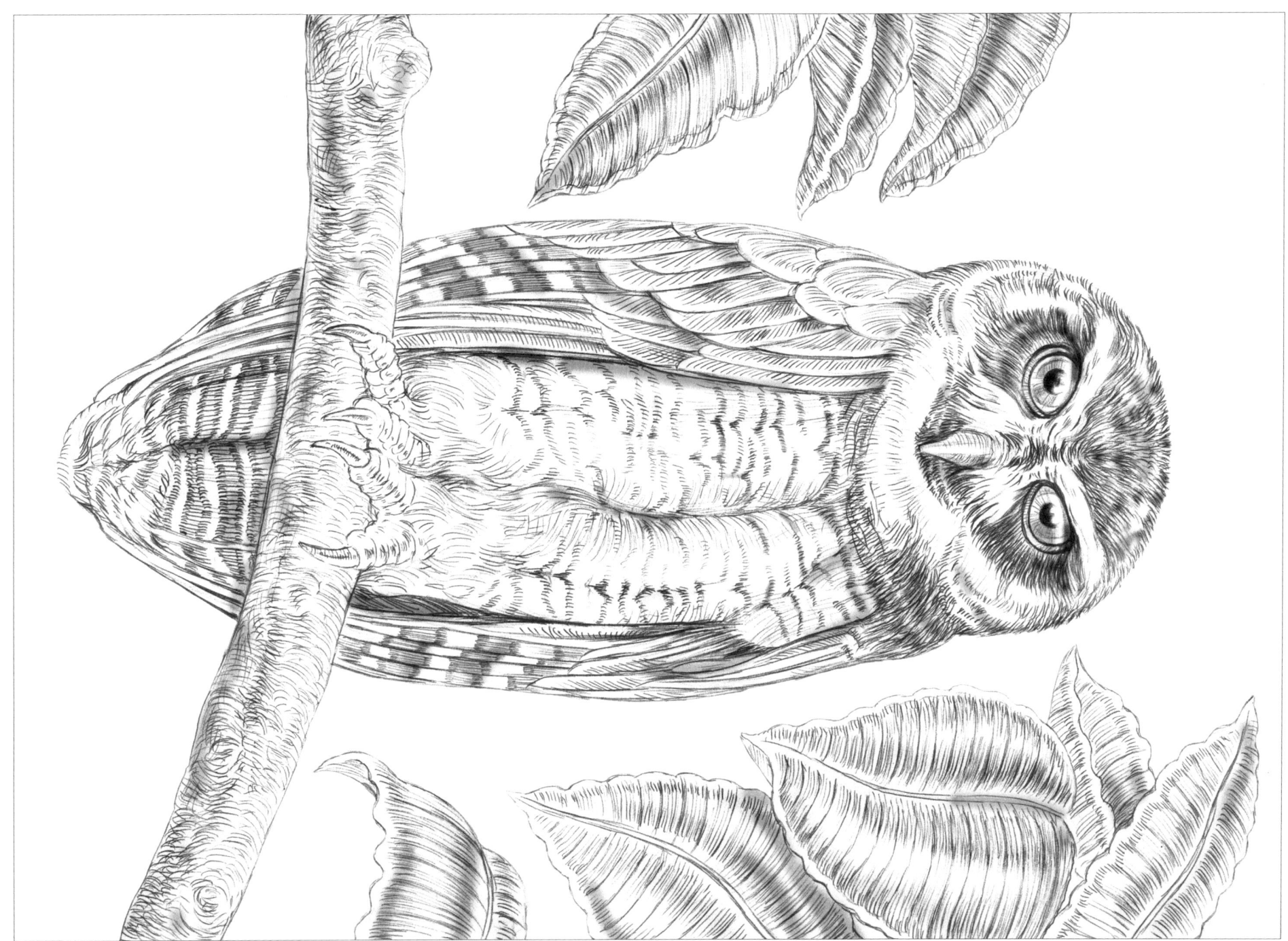

Spectacled Owl

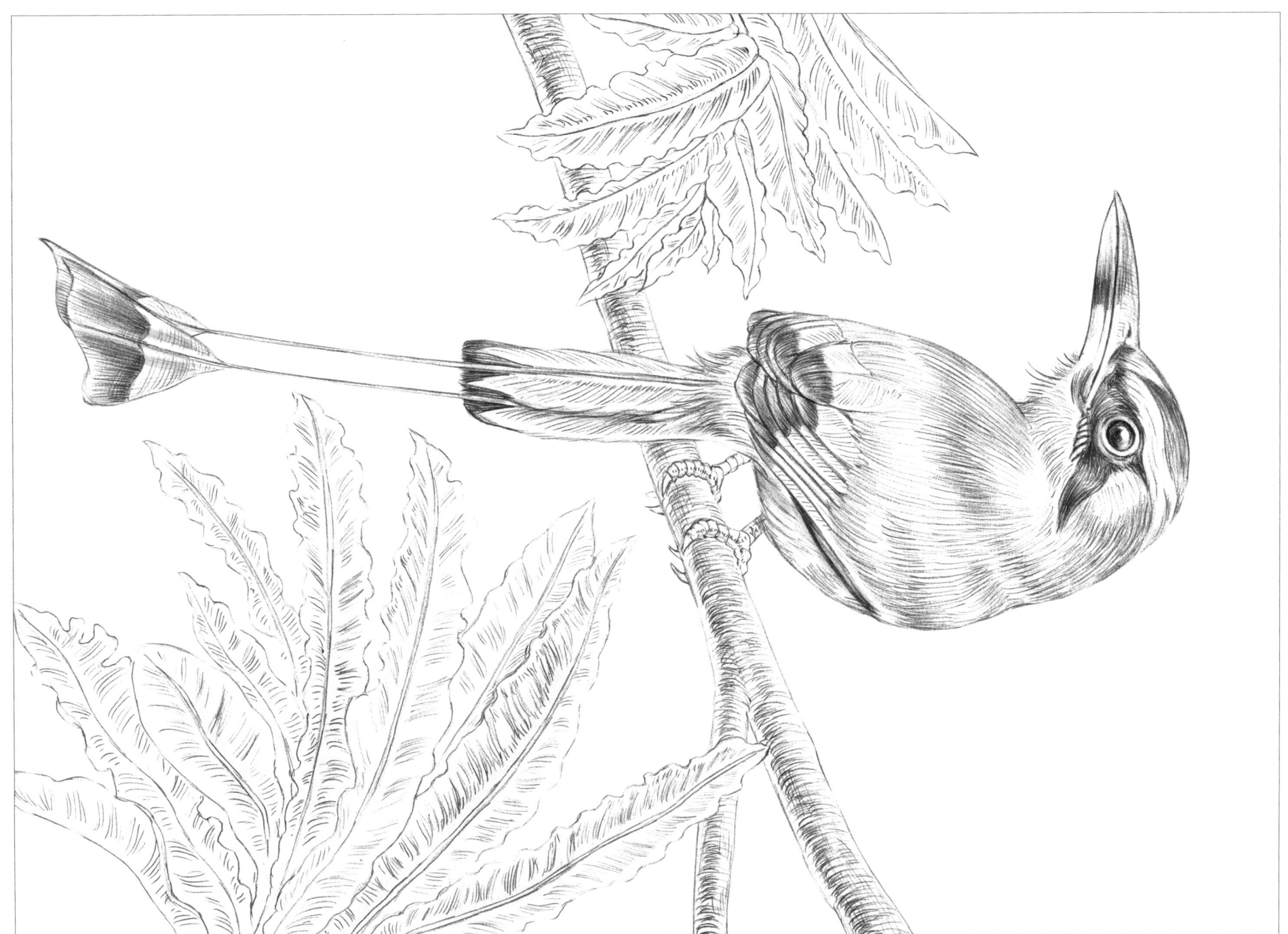

Turquoise-Browed Motmot

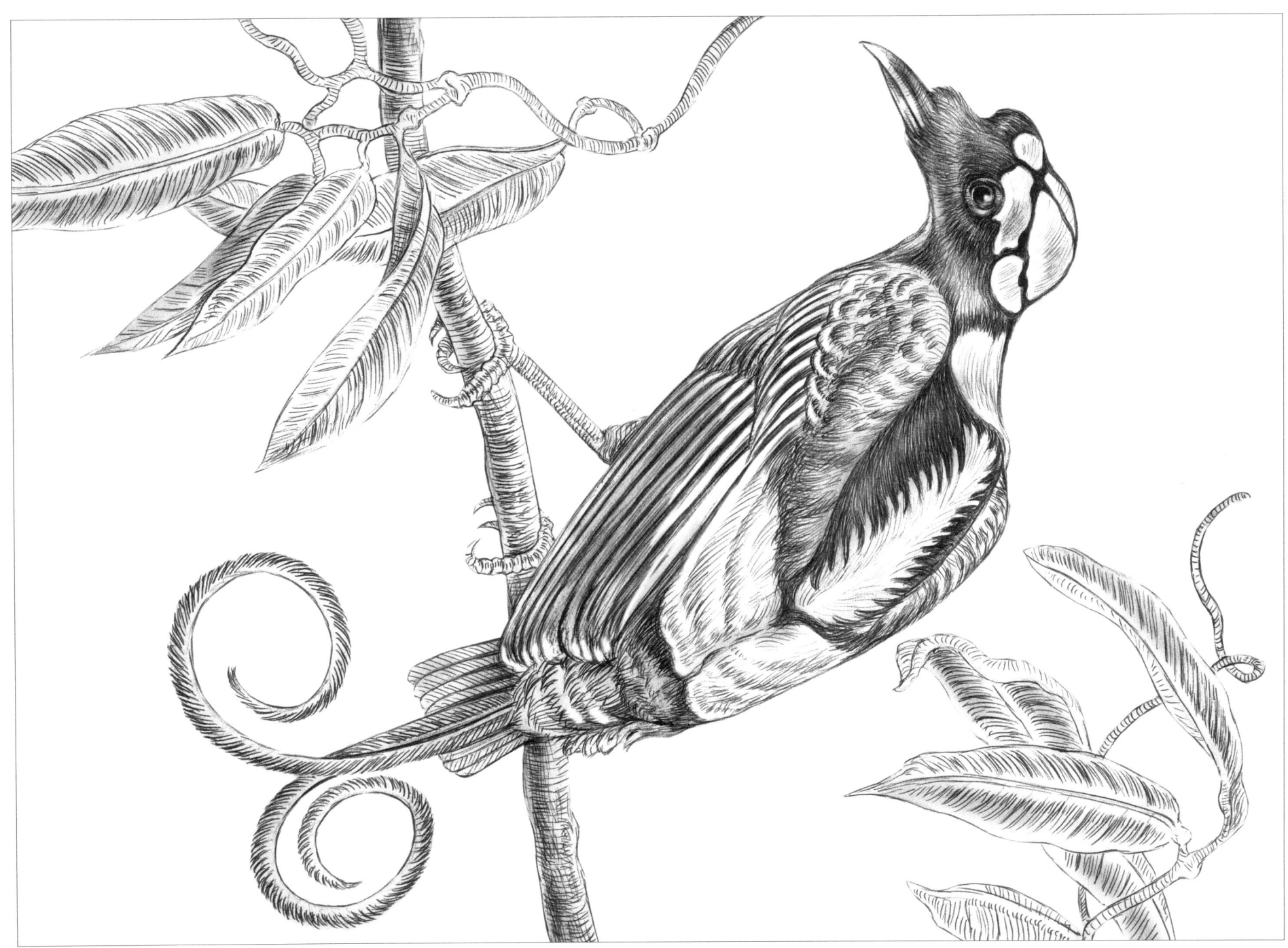

Wilson's Bird-of-Paradise

**Tim Jeffs** is a New York City based artist and illustrator who has been creating dynamic artwork for over 25 years. Animals are a favorite subject matter of his, along with the complex and intricate details these creatures possess. *"The incredible diversity and complexity of animals has always intrigued me. They offer endless pleasure to look and marvel upon. In every drawing I try to capture the unique quality of each particular animal. I hope you enjoy my perspective, love and admiration of these incredible creatures."*

Visit my website for prints, digital coloring books and coloring lessons:

## www.TimJeffsArt.com

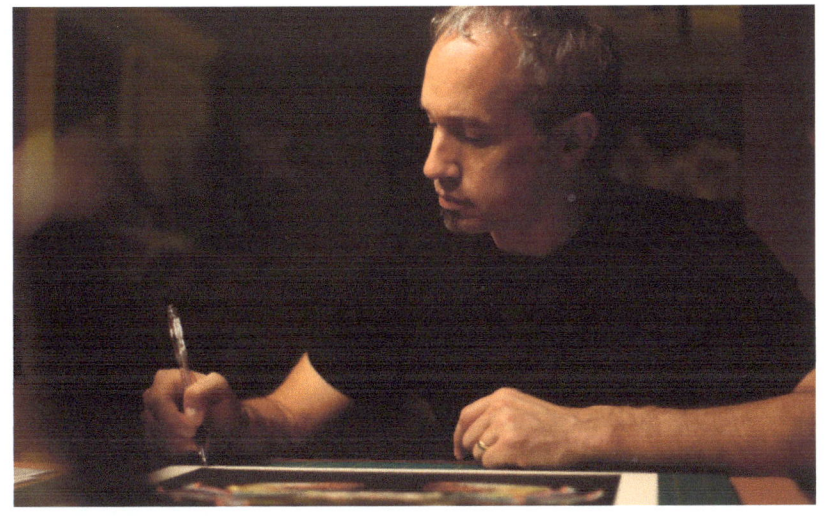

# Discover the full line of Tim Jeffs' Published Coloring Books

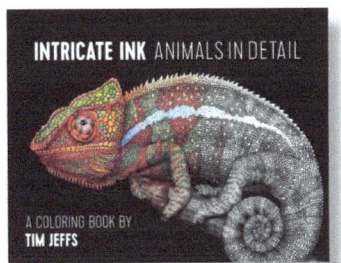 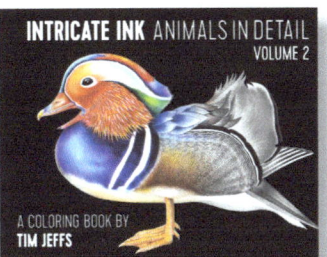 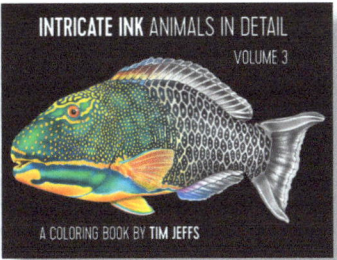 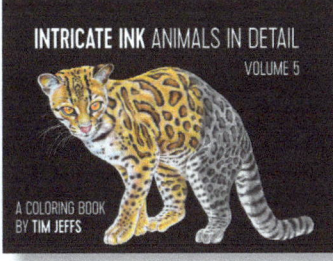 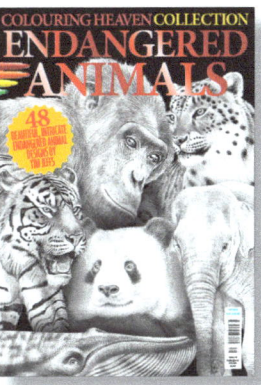

**Intricate Ink Animals In Detail Volume 1, 2 3 and 5** Available at:
Pomegranate.com
Amazon.com
Bookdepository.com

**Colouring Heaven Collection
Endangered Animals**
Available at: Colouringheaven.com

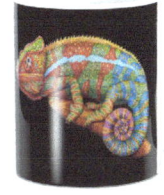

# Discover Tim Jeffs' Merchandise

**Etsy Shop**
www.etsy.com/shop/TimJeffsArt

**Society6 Shop**
www.society6.com/TimJeffsArt

**Redbubble Shop**
TimJeffsArt.redbubble.com

**Vsual Print Shop**
https://vsual.co/shop/tim-jeffs-art

# Discover the full line of Tim Jeffs Digital Coloring Books at:
## www.TimJeffsArt.com

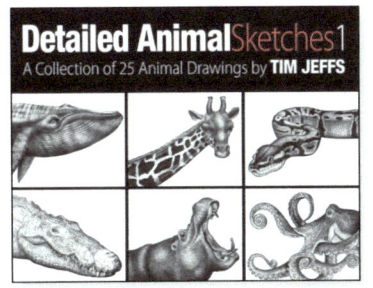 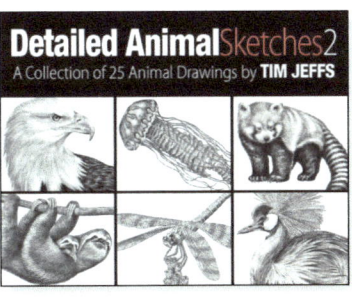 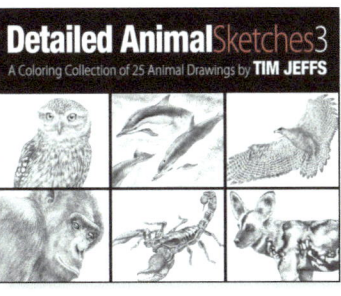 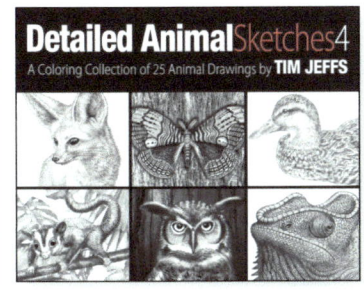 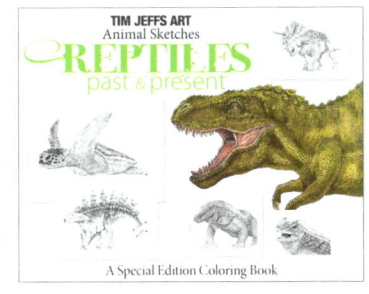

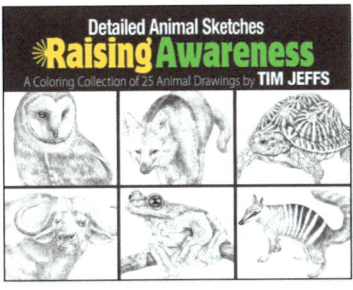 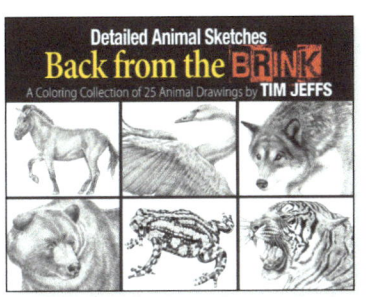 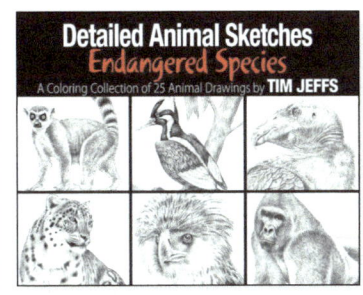 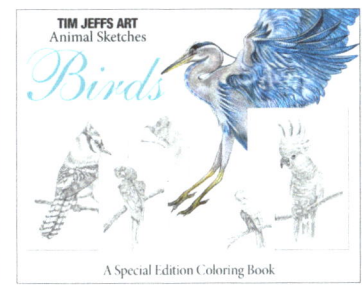 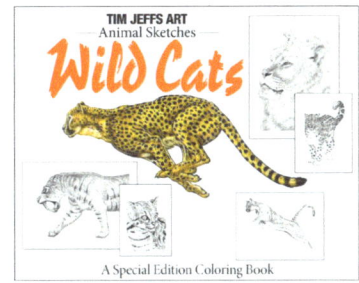

## And Coloring Lessons

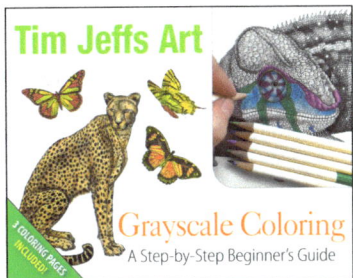 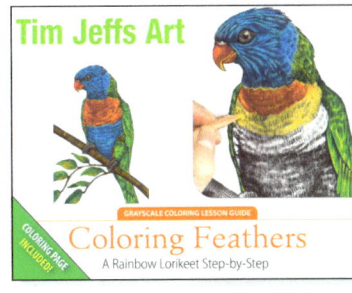 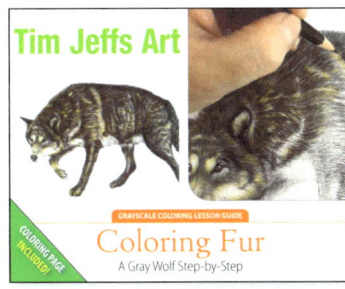 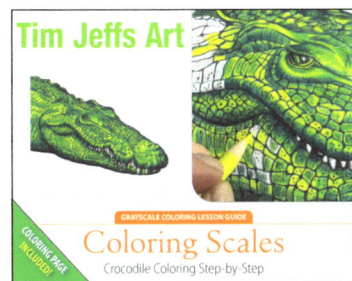 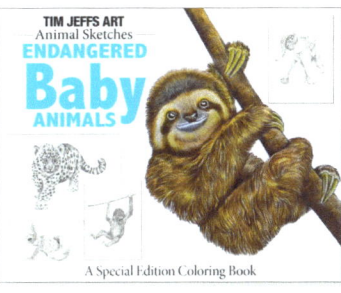

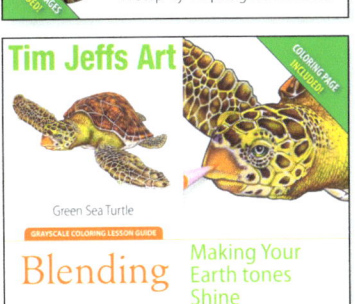 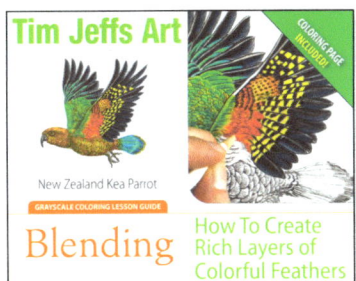 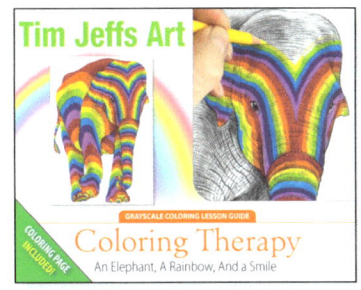 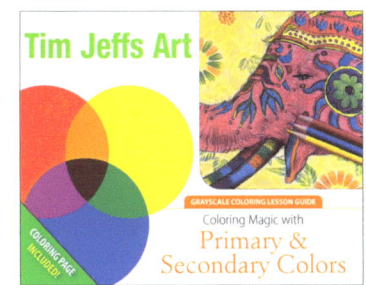 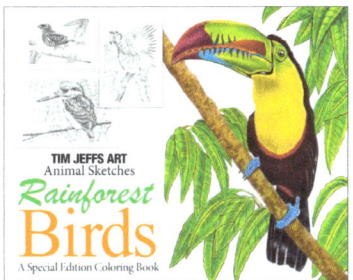

# TIM JEFFS ART  Online Resources

## Share Your Creativity with the World!

Join the ever-expanding coloring group of animal lovers who inspire each other through their colorings of the animals from Tim's books and lessons. With thousands of members from all around the world, Tim's Facebook group "Intricate Ink Coloring Group" is a creative and safe space where everyone is welcome. Jo Warren, the groups all-inspiring administrator will welcome you in with open arms and is there to encourage everyone to just have fun no matter your coloring skill level. Come join, we can't wait to have you as a member! Join Tim's Facebook Coloring Group at:

**www.facebook.com/groups/intricateink**

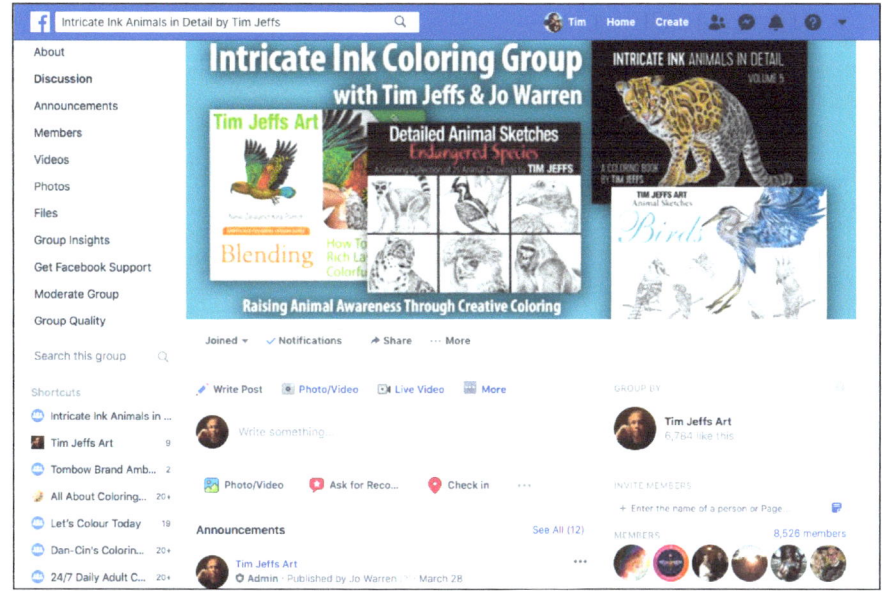

## Visit the Home of Tim Jeffs Art

**TimJeffsArt.com** is my home on the web where I display all of my work and various projects. I hope you can stop by for a visit! You'll find my new shop where signed and unsigned prints of all of my animal drawings are available to purchase, along with the complete library of my digital download coloring books and grayscale coloring lessons. In the conservation section, you can see the projects that I am very proud of. Using my art to preserve wildlife is so important to me.

**www.TimJeffsArt.com**

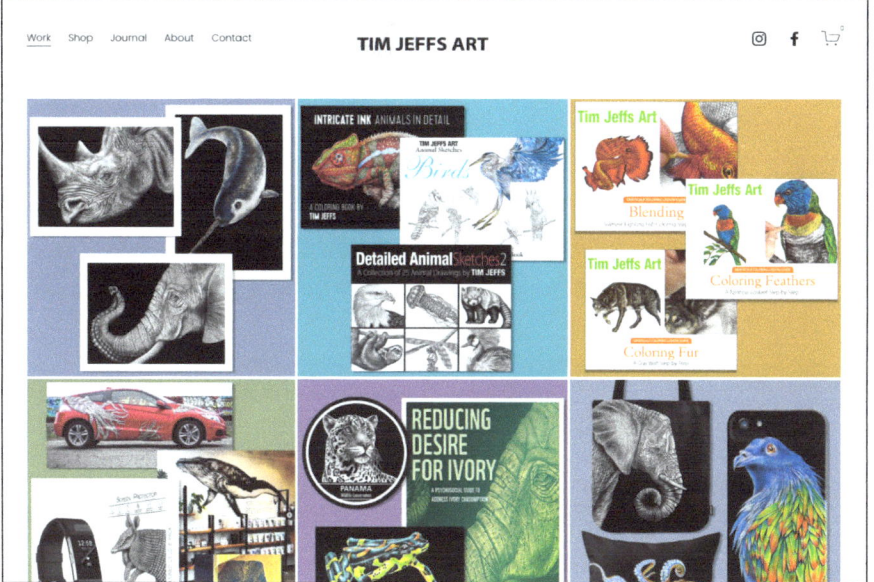